# Nelson Grammar International Pupil Book 2

## Contents

| | | |
|---|---|---|
| Unit 1 | Alphabetical order | 2 |
| Unit 2 | Naming words | 4 |
| Unit 3 | More than one | 6 |
| Unit 4 | Doing words | 8 |
| Unit 5 | Describing words | 10 |
| Unit 6 | Naming words and describing words | 12 |
| Check-up 1 | Units 1–6 | 14 |
| Unit 7 | Writing sentences | 16 |
| Unit 8 | Questions | 18 |
| Unit 9 | Naming words | 20 |
| Unit 10 | Doing words | 22 |
| Unit 11 | Special naming words | 24 |
| Unit 12 | Writing sentences | 26 |
| Unit 13 | Describing words | 28 |
| Check-up 2 | Units 7–13 | 30 |

# Unit 1: Alphabetical order

> **TIP**
> This is how we write small letters.

These letters are in **alphabetical order**.

a b c d e f g h i j k l m
n o p q r s t u v w x y z

Look at the first letter of each of these words.

**a**pple **b**ook **c**at

The words are in alphabetical order. The first letters are in the order that they appear in the alphabet.

## Focus

> **TIP**
> Use the alphabet at the top of the page to help you.

Put these groups of letters in **alphabetical order**. Write them in your book.

1. b c a
2. f e g
3. k l j
4. o n p
5. u t s
6. y w x

2

# Practice

Write these words in **alphabetical order**.
Look at the first letter of each word.

1. bell    ant    can    doll

2. lips 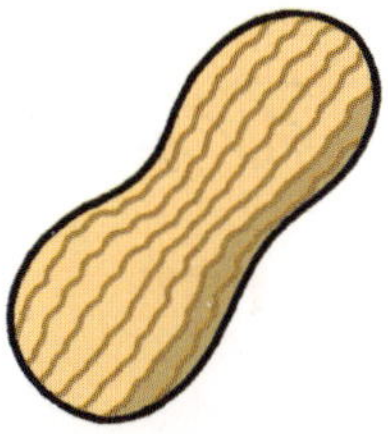   nut    key    mop

3. jelly    hat    ice    kick

4. umbrella    van 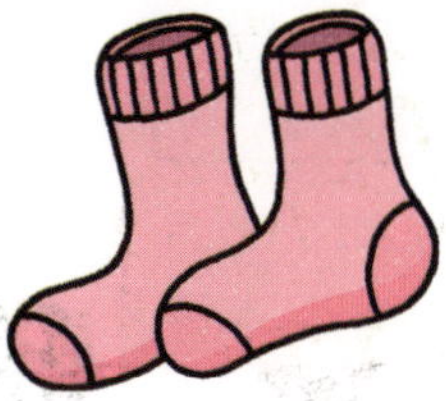   socks    tap

# Extension

Which word comes **first** in a dictionary?

1. cook   or   book
2. sip   or   tip
3. met   or   net

# Unit 2 Naming words

The words below are **naming words**.
They tell us the names of things.

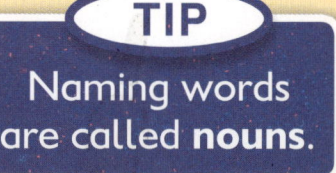
TIP
Naming words are called **nouns**.

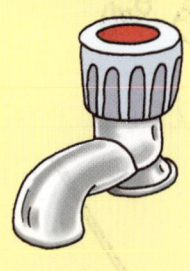   

tap        sun        rat        crab

## Focus

Add a letter to finish each of these **naming words**.
Write the words in your book.

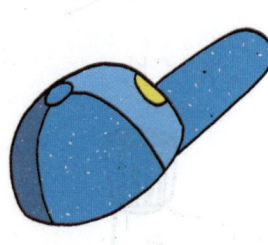   

1  ca__        3  p__n

2  v__n        4  __an

 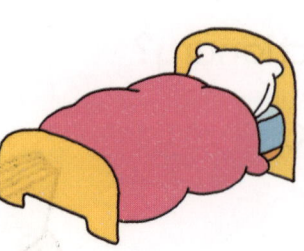  

5  je__        7  __in

6  b__d        8  he__

## Practice

Copy the **naming words**.
Tick the words you can see in the picture.

1. log   2. cat   3. mop   4. sun
5. hut   6. man   7. van   8. fan

## Extension

Write four **naming words** you can see in this picture.

# Unit 3 More than one

**TIP**
Singular means one.
Plural means more than one.

We add 's' to lots of words when we mean **more than one**.

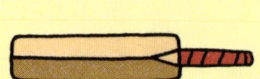  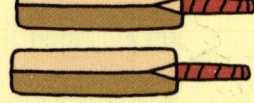       

one bat        two bat**s**        one ball         five ball**s**

## Focus

What are the missing words that go with these pictures? Write them in your book.

**1** one hill   two _____

**2** one cup   three _____

**3** one duck   four  _____    **4** one log   five _____

6

## Practice

Write what you can see in each picture.

**1** two ........    **2** five ........    **3** three ........

## Extension

Look at the words below.
Copy the words that mean **more than one**.

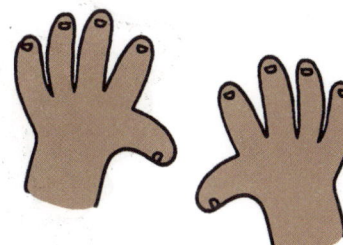

legs    pet

bat     hands

tents   rocks

jug     bells

hill    bulls

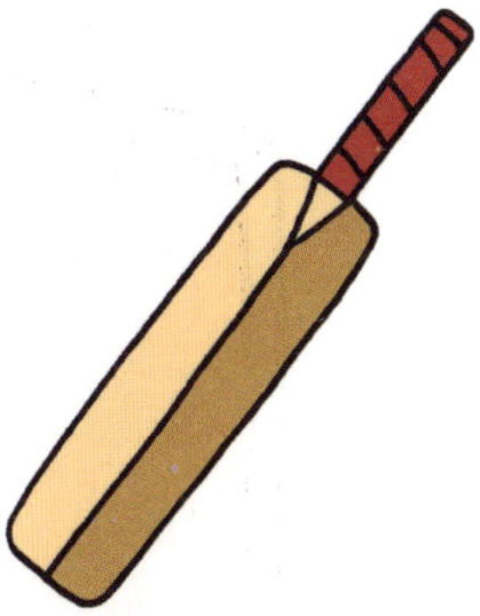

# Unit 4: Doing words

The words below are **doing words**.

The girl **throws** the ball.    The boy **hits** the ball.

> **TIP**
> Doing words are called **verbs**.

## Focus

Write the **doing words** in your book.

1. The bull chases the man.

2. The girl bangs the door.

3. The monkey climbs the tree.

# Practice

Write the correct **doing word** for each picture.

**1** feeding   sleeping    **2** walking   skipping

**3** rushing   fishing    **4** dripping   drumming

# Extension

Write a sentence to show what is being done in each picture.

**1**    **2**    **3**

## Unit 5: Describing words

**Describing words** tell us more about a person or thing.

> **TIP:** Describing words are called **adjectives**.

The **long** snake is hiding behind the **grey** rock.

## Focus

Write the **describing words** in your book.

> **TIP:** Number 4 has two **describing words**.

1  The red flag is flying today.

2  The small boy is crying.

3  The big box is hard to lift.

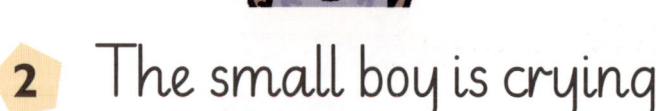

4  The dirty coat and muddy boots are on the floor.

## Practice

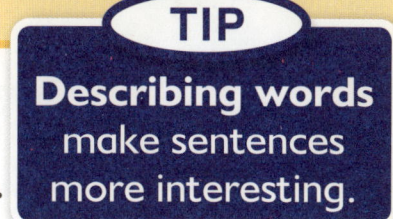

**TIP**
Describing words make sentences more interesting.

Copy the sentences below.
Add **describing words** of your own to finish them.

**1** The .......... sun is setting over the .......... sea.

**2** The .......... giraffe is eating the .......... leaves.

**3** The .......... clouds are covering the .......... moon.

**4** The .......... rabbit is hiding behind the .......... trees.

## Extension

Copy the six **describing words** in this box.

| thin | bed | short | pretty | cat | small |
| log | pink | list | shell | old | |

11

# Unit 6: Naming words and describing words

**TIP** A **describing word** tells us about a **naming word**.

The red words below are **naming words**. They tell us the names of things.

a **tent**     a **man**

The red words below are **describing words**. They tell us more about a person or thing.

a **red** tent

an **old** man

## Focus

Match a **naming word** with a **describing word** for each picture. Write the pairs of words in your book.

1

2

3

4

| Naming words | Describing words |
|---|---|
| hands   flower | long   happy |
| clown   ladder | cold   yellow |

## Practice

**TIP** A **naming word** tells us the name of something.

Copy the **naming words** from these sentences.

1. This is a green bag.
2. Can you see the white bird?
3. Where is the little duck?
4. Get a warm hat.
5. He is a thin man.

## Extension

**TIP** A **describing word** tells us more about a **naming word**.

Copy the **describing words** from these sentences.

1. The hot drink is ready.
2. This is a long road.
3. The black cat is lost.
4. This is a wet mop.
5. Can you see the large clouds?

13

# Check-up 1

## Alphabetical order

Put each of these groups of words into **alphabetical order**.

1. sell   queen   rock   trick
2. log   jump   kick   men
3. owl   mop   pen   not
4. van   well   ten   up

## Naming words

Copy the **naming words** from each list.

1. is   pin   sock   bus
2. jug   cup   his   at
3. not   pen   bed   bat
4. bad   man   an   leg
5. fed   wet   peg   hill

## More than one

Look at the words below.
Copy the words that mean **more than one**.

rings   cots   click   snails
king   bells   mill   cups
neck   locks   hats   door

14

## Doing words

Copy the **doing word** from each sentence.

1. The seal swims in the sea.
2. The fox drinks the water.
3. The snake hisses at the man.
4. The mouse nibbles the cheese.
5. The spider spins the web.

## Describing words

Copy the **describing words** from each list.

1. peg   red   tidy   bed
2. old   cot   sad   long
3. pet   ten   green   fog
4. hot   child   box   cold
5. thin   mug   happy   bun

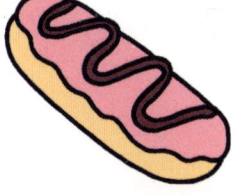

# Unit 7 Writing sentences

**TIP** Sentences must make sense.

A **sentence** starts with a **capital letter** and usually ends with a **full stop**.

**M**eena is waiting for the bus**.**

**I**t is raining**.**

**S**he is very wet**.**

## Focus

**A** Copy these **sentences** into your book. Put rings around the **capital letters** and **full stops**.

1 Chad looked at the clock.

2 My pen has run out of ink.

**B** Copy these sentences and add the missing capital letters and full stops.

1 my cat sleeps on my bed

2 lee gave his mum a hug

# Practice

Look at the pictures.
Write a new **sentence** about each picture.

1

2

3

4

5

6

# Extension

Put these words in the right order to make a **sentence**.

read    book.    have
   I       not       this

**TIP**
Make sure the sentence starts with a **capital letter** and ends with a **full stop**.

17

# Unit 8 Questions

Some sentences **tell us something**.
Telling sentences end with a **full stop**.

Some sentences **ask us something**.
Asking sentences end with a **question mark**.

It is windy today.

Is it windy today?

Asking sentences are called **questions**.

## Focus

**TIP** Look for the question marks.

Copy the **questions** into your book.

Where are you going?
I am going to the shops.
What are you going to buy?
I am going to buy apples.
Will you get some oranges too?
We have oranges in the bowl.

# Practice

Copy these sentences.
End the telling sentences with a **full stop**.
End the asking sentences with a **question mark**.

1. Will you stay for tea
2. Is it ready now
3. Do you like cheese
4. I like to drink milk
5. Can I help you
6. I love the cake

# Extension

Finish these **questions**.

1. What is ...................................
2. Why does ...............................
3. When can ...............................
4. Where are ...............................
5. Who will ...............................

# Unit 9 Naming words

**Naming words** tell us the names of things.

tree

book

ship

**TIP**
Naming words are called **nouns**.

## Focus

**A** What are the **naming words** for these pictures? Write the words in your book.

1  b _ _          2  b _ _ _          3  n _ _ _ _

4  s _ _ _          5  f _ _ _          6  k _ _ _

**B** Look at the clothes you have on. Write three **naming words** you see.

# Practice

Look at this picture.

Copy the sentences below.
Finish them using **naming words** from the box.

> cake    castle    sea    chair    ball

1. Two people are playing with a ............................
2. Andrew is making a ............................
3. Dad is eating a ............................
4. Tom is asleep in the ............................
5. There is a boat on the ............................

# Extension

Write four more **naming words** you can see in the picture.

# Unit 10 Doing words

**TIP** Doing words are called **verbs.**

**Doing words** tell us what people and animals are doing.

The boy **feeds** the bird.

The bird **pecks** the ground.

Doing words also tell us what things are doing.

The wind **blows**.   The tree **bends**.   The leaves **fall**.

## Focus

What are these things doing? Choose a **doing word** from the box for each picture. Write the words in your book.

dripping   shining   falling
flying    sleeping   drinking

1 ................

2 ................

3 ................

4 ................

5 ................

6 ................

# Practice

Look at the pictures below. Use a **doing word** from the box to answer each question. The first one is done for you.

bouncing   banging   ringing
swinging   falling

**1**   What is the door doing?

_banging_

**2**   What is the rain doing?

_____

**3**   What is the bell doing?

_____

**4**   What is the ball doing?

_____

**5**   What is the swing doing?

_____

# Extension

Write all the **doing words** you can do with your legs. How many can you think of?

walking, skipping ...

# Unit 11: Special naming words

**TIP** Special naming words are called **proper nouns**.

**Special naming words** begin with a **capital letter**.
Names of people are special naming words.
Names of pets are special naming words.

**Mrs Brown** has two cats. They are called **Sandy** and **Mandy**.

## Focus

Find the **special naming words** in each sentence. Write them in your book.

1. My pony is called Lucky.

2. Dillon the parrot is owned by Mr Kasim.

3. Sue has a hamster called Bunty.

4. Fuzz the cat loves to chase mice.

5. Annie the goat likes to eat clothes.

# Practice

Use **special naming words** to answer these questions.

1. What is your first name?
2. What is your last name?
3. What is your teacher's name?
4. What is your friend's name?

# Extension

**TIP** Remember the **capital letters**.

Look at this picture.

Rose    Jessica    Sanjay    Rory

Use **special naming words** to answer each question.

1. Who lives at number 3?
2. Who lives at number 2?
3. Who lives at number 4?
4. Who lives at number 1?
5. Who has a parrot?
6. Who has a cat?

# Unit 12 Writing sentences

**TIP** Sentences must make sense.

**Telling sentences** end with a **full stop**.

The car is stuck in the mud.

**Asking sentences** end with a **question mark**.

Have I missed the train?

## Focus

Copy the sentences below into your book.
End the telling sentences with a **full stop**.
End the asking sentences with a **question mark**.

1. What time is it
2. I am late for school
3. Did you eat your breakfast
4. What did you have
5. I had tea and toast
6. Where is my school bag

## Practice

Look at this picture.

 **A** Write four **telling sentences** about the picture.

**TIP**
Remember the full stops and question marks.

 **B** Look at the picture again.
Write four **asking sentences** about the picture.

## Extension

Asking sentences are called **questions**. Write a possible question to each of these answers.

1. My favourite radio show.
2. We are leaving at 6 o'clock.
3. Chess club is on Tuesday.
4. We are having pizza and chips for tea.

27

# Unit 13 Describing words

**TIP** Describing words are called **adjectives**.

**Describing words** tell us more about a person or a thing. Describing words make sentences more interesting.

We can write about the picture like this:

The waves tossed the ship.

This is a more interesting sentence, using describing words.

The **huge** waves tossed the **battered** ship.

## Focus

Choose a **describing word** from the box to make each sentence more interesting. Write the sentences in your book.

old    muddy    little    wooden

1 The book is torn.

2 The man climbs out of the ditch.

3 The fire is burning the house.

4 The kitten has hurt itself.

28

## Practice

Use **describing words** of your own to make these sentences more interesting.

1. The balloon is in the sky.
2. The tiger lives in the jungle.
3. The man has a stick. 
4. The boy is making a tree house.

## Extension

Copy and finish these sentences with two **describing words**.

1. The _____, _____ snake lay in the sun. 
2. My _____, _____ coat needs a wash.
3. The _____, _____ car raced to the finish line.

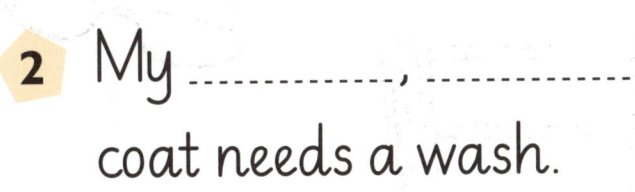

# Check-up 2

## Writing sentences

Copy these **sentences**.
Add the **capital letters** and **full stops**.

1 he will go to see the football match

2 there is no post today

3 here is the book you wanted

## Questions

Which of these are **questions**?
Write the questions with **question marks**.

1 Is it cold

2 The weather is fine

3 Will I need an umbrella

## Naming words

Write the **naming words** from each of these sentences.

1. Put the cup on the table.

2. I have my book and pen.

3. Can you find the shoes?

## Doing words

Write a sentence using each of these **doing words**.

1. walk

2. hunts

3. eat

4. shouts

5. write

6. runs

## Special naming words

Write the **special naming words** with **capital letters**.

| | | |
|---|---|---|
| wave | greg | barn |
| george | card | mrs pope |
| akram | nita | parrot |
| mr lee | kim | farm |

## Describing words

**A** Write the **describing words** from these sentences.

1. This is a steep hill.
2. These are hard sums.
3. It is a dark night.

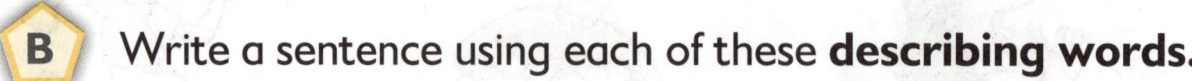

**B** Write a sentence using each of these **describing words**.

1. small
2. tall
3. fresh
4. best
5. dusty
6. flat

32